GOD
is
Love

I John 4:8b

Dr. Lisa H. Fuller

Published by

Learn Realistic Habits for the Future

Published by:

Learn Realistic Habits for the Future

ISBN: 978-0-9754023-1-3

Manufactured in the United States of America

Cover and Interior Design by: Christina Dixon

Dedication:

God,
thank you for your love!

God,

I pray that each person reading this book is blessed. I ask you to protect them and their families. Keep them safe both at home and at school.

In the name of Jesus,

Amen

God is love.

I John 4:8b

The Bible is a Holy Book.

God speaks to us and tells us who He is through the Bible.

Writings found in the Bible are called Holy Scriptures.

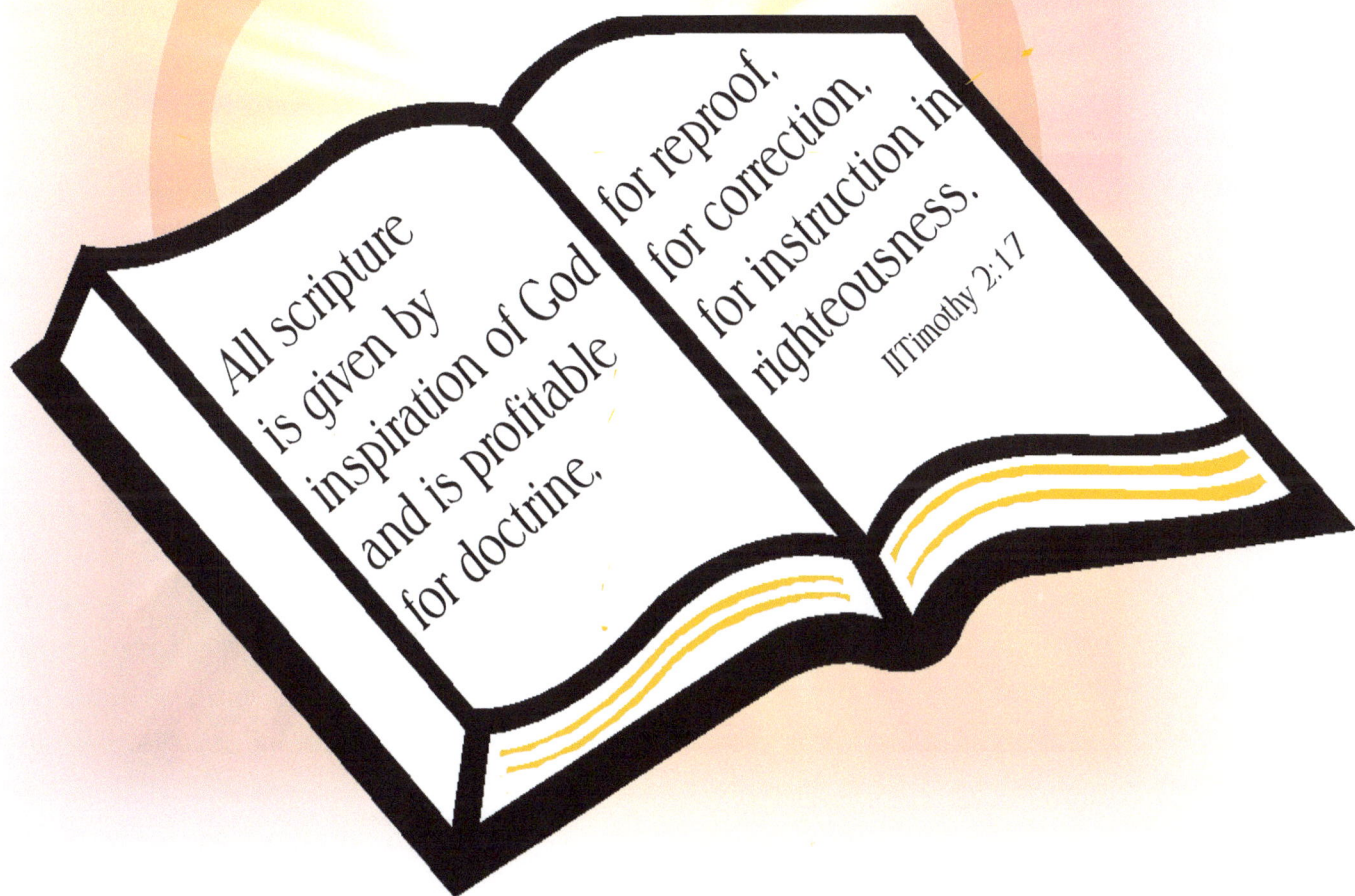

All scripture is given by inspiration of God and is profitable for doctrine, for reproof, for correction, for instruction in righteousness.

IITimothy 2:17

Holy Scriptures tell us that...

In the beginning God created the heavens and the earth.

Genesis 1:1

God is the Creator of the universe and that God is love.

God loves us and wants us to love Him.

God wants us to love each other.

When we do bad things such as disobeying our parents, stealing, lying, cheating, killing, or being mean to each other, we commit wrongdoings against God.

These wrongdoings are called

SINS

God does not like sin.

$$\frac{GOD}{SIN} \neq$$

Sin separates us from God.

GOD

SIN

God loves us and wants to be with us.

God sent Jesus to pay the punishment for our sins by dying on the cross for us.

On the third day, Jesus rose from the grave.

Today,

Jesus sits at the right hand of God in heaven.

The Bible says in St. John Chapter 3 verse 16

For God so loved the world, that he gave his only begotten Son, that whosoever believeth in him should not perish, but have everlasting life.

St. John 3:16

This is how we know that God loves us.

Do you want Jesus to pay the price for your sins?

Do you want to accept Jesus as Lord and Savior over your life?

Say the next page aloud.

I believe in my heart that Jesus is the Son of God. I believe that Jesus died on the cross and rose from the grave. I accept Jesus as Lord and Savior over my life.

Now you are no longer separated from God.

GOD

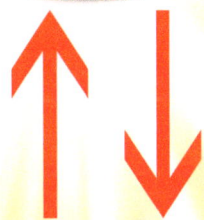

you

God is love!

He that loveth not knoweth not God; for God is love.

I John 4:8

Prayer:

God,

I thank You for each person that accepts Your Son Jesus as Lord and Savior and receives forgiveness of their sins.

Give them assurance that Jesus is Lord. Let them know that You are Love.

Amen

ABOUT THE AUTHOR

Dr. Lisa H. Fuller

Dr. Lisa H. Fuller is a licensed minister of the Gospel of Jesus Christ. She is an international lecturer, author, teacher, counselor, and psychiatrist.

Dr. Fuller is available for book readings, book signings, and presentations.

Contact information

Website: LisaHFullerMinistries.org
Email: LisaHFullerMinistries@gmail.com
Facebook: LisaHFullerMinistries
Phone: (313) 398-3131

Products:

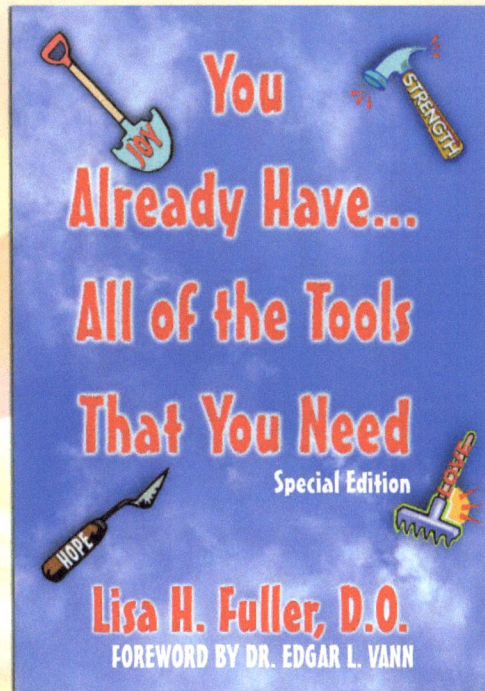

You Already Have
All of the Tools that You Need (Book)

www.ingramcontent.com/pod-product-compliance
Lightning Source LLC
Chambersburg PA
CBHW041544040426
42447CB00002B/41

* 9 7 8 0 9 7 5 4 0 2 3 1 3 *